THE CONTROLLING POWER OF THE MIND
Renewing Your Mind Unto Victory

The Controlling Power Of The Mind

The Controlling Power Of The Mind: Renewing Your Mind Unto Victory

All Rights Reserved

Copyright © 2016 by Gabriel Amoateng-Boahen

No part of this publication may be reproduced, stored in a retrieval system or transmitted in any way by any means, electronic, mechanical, photocopy, digital imaging, recording or otherwise, without the prior written permission of the author who is the copyright owner, except as provided by USA copyright law.

Bible references are taken from the various translations of the Bible as stated.

Author's Contact: *gabriel.ab925@yahoo.com*
gabrielabm1913@gmail.com

First Printed in July 2016

The opinions expressed by the author in this book are not necessarily those of Rehoboth House.

Paperback: 7
Hardcover: 978-1-68411-024-7

Published in the United States of America by
Rehoboth House, Chicago.
www.rehobothhouseonline.com

REHOBOTH HOUSE

The Controlling Power Of The Mind

Table of Contents

Dedication ix
Acknowledgment xi
Preface xiii
Abstract xv
Introduction xxi

Chapter 1
The Power Of The Mind
The Mind Controls the Whole Body 1
Negative Thoughts And Failure 2
Positive Thoughts And Holistic Healing 2
Physical and Spiritual Failures 3
Positive Confession Leads to Victory 4

Chapter 2
Potentiality Maximization
Full Utilization of The Mind Power 7
Education (Informal and Formal) and Intellectuality 8
Sound Mind and the "Beautiful City" 11

Chapter 3
The Mind Controls The Environment
Afforestation or Desertification Is a Choice of The Mind 13
Individuals, Families, Communities, And Nations Make A "Mind-Choice" 14
Marriage And Family 14
Nations 14
The Story/Plight of Poor and Rich Nations 16
Basic Principles Of Ethics 17
Professionals Take Over With Best Choices 18
Clean And Healthy Water Is Good Medicine For The Human Body 19
Five Tips To Help You Drink More 21
Conclusion 23

Chapter 4
Nations Are Developed By Brains, Not Natural Resources
Abundant Natural Resources..25
Excellent Human Resources..26
The Brain Takes The Lead..26
Each Benefits From the Other...27
To Achieve Holistic Development..27

Chapter 5
Divine Power Is Supreme
The Brain is Central to Development...31
The Pen is Mightier Than the Sword..32
What The Brain Can See and Do..32
Renewal and Transformation (Rom. 12:1-2) 33
On The Road To Victory..34

Conclusion..35

Prayer Of Salvation..39

Prayer Of Rededication..41

All On Fire Brethren..43

Recommended Books..45

Blurb...49

Author's Profile...51

DEDICATION

Dedicated to my eldest and first-ever Christian daughter, Mrs. Rebecca Obeng and husband, Pastor Samuel Obeng, of the Anchor of Hope International Ministries, Bronx, New York, USA. I travelled from Chicago to visit Pastor and Mrs. Samuel Obeng and family from April 22- 26, 2016. As I flew back and reflected on the pastoral visit to encourage them in ministry, the Holy Spirit dropped the book title into my spirit. It therefore stands to reason, and more appropriate, to dedicate this "mind-driven" book in their honor; and also to appreciate them dearly and sincerely for their encouragement and support during my theological and ministerial studies in the US. My passion to establish the Royal Diadem Pastoral Center in Kumasi, Ghana, was confirmed when Pastor and Mrs. Samuel Obeng whole-heartedly and freely donated their large plot of land to me for the construction work to begin. I am forever grateful and thankful to Pastor Sam and Lady Becky.

ACKNOWLEDGMENT

I wish to acknowledge and appreciate the immense contribution of educators, psychologists, psychiatrists, and all those who work and help the mentally-challenged, especially, special education teachers at the Kenwood Academy High School, Chicago, Illinois, USA.

PREFACE

My many years of counseling and companioning people in ministry, and my own personal experiences, motivated me to write this book to unveil and expose what the enemy is doing in the "dark room" of the unseen human part called the mind. Great ideas and accomplishments, physical healing, emotional healing, divine/spiritual healing, marvelous exploits, and inventions are released when the "mind closet" is unlocked. The freed-mind is limitless, and in terms of successes and accomplishments, the sky is even lower in exploitation. The mind can either imprison or liberate the individual. The mind as a matter of fact, is the "battlefield" where fights of positivity and negativity are in continued confrontation. The source of peace or war, good or evil, is the mind. It takes the Word of God to free the mind, so Apostle Paul pleaded.

> "I beseech you therefore, brethren, by the mercies of God, that ye present your bodies a living sacrifice, holy, acceptable unto God, which is your reasonable service. And be not conformed to this world: but be ye transformed by the renewing of your mind, that ye may prove what is that good, and acceptable, and perfect, will of God" (Romans 12:1-2).

This book among others, presents some very interesting, intellectual, and logical arguments for the reflection of the reader. For example, I made statements like: family and community conflicts and even world wars begin in the mind at the round-table International Conference Rooms; that no one should underrate the controlling power of the mind. In other words, the mind controls the environment. Desertification or afforestation (Afforestation is the establishment of a forest or stand of trees in an area where there was no forest) / reforestation (Reforestation is the establishment of forest cover, either naturally (by natural seeding, coppice, or root suckers) or artificially (by direct seeding or planting) is the product of the mind.

The pen is the product of the mind; new inventions have evolved and taken over the old ways of doing things through the power of the mind-sending urgent messages through telegrams from Chicago to Kintampo, Ghana, have given way to faxing same messages, electronic mails, or telephone. I made a case and defended it when I said that "abundant natural resources do not necessarily develop a nation but best brains." I also quoted Dr. Myles Munroe, a renowned international preacher from the Bahamas, who has already gone ahead of us to be with the Lord in heaven, when he once said that **"The greatest tragedy in life is not death, but a life without a purpose."** He further amplifies my point of emphasis in relation to the mind when he also said that **"Solid character will reflect itself in consistent behavior, while poor character will seek to hide behind deceptive words and actions… When purpose is not known, abuse is inevitable… You must decide if you are going to rob the world or bless it with the rich, valuable, potent, untapped resources locked away within you."**

This is a book you cannot afford missing reading it to the end. The ideas raised juxtapose and balance Christian conduct and spirituality with economic and environmental development from both the "micro and macro" perspectives. Persistency is key in mind development, and therefore, I agree with James N. Watkins who once said, **"a river is able to cut through a rock not because it is powerful, but because of its persistence."**

Find the answer to this "revelational question" from my book: What is the wealthiest place in the world in relation to the mind?

ABSTRACT

The brain is central to human development. Though hidden, it has such a great power of influence, either positively or negatively. Behind the tall magnificent complex architectural buildings in downtown Chicago are best brains at work on the drawing board, and also true for the complexities of network of roads, air travel, and large ships on the deep blue sea. To talk about the pen is to talk about the mind. The pen is the product of the mind-movement from the papyrus plant tree era, to scrolls, fountain pen and ink era, then to ball-point pens, and now to desktop computers, laptops, tablets, and other forms of writing to keep records and information. Abundant natural resources alone do not necessarily develop a nation but best and continuous renewing minds/brains through evaluation and re-evaluation, orientation, in-service training, refresher courses, annual reviews, and renewal of professional certificates, and other official licenses and documentations.

INTRODUCTION

The Genesis of the Book Title

Through many years of counseling and companioning people in ministry, and my own personal experiences in life, led me to write this book to unveil and also to expose what the enemy is doing in the "dark room" of the unseen human part called the mind. Great ideas and accomplishments, physical healing, divine healing, marvelous exploits, and inventions are released when the "mind closet" is unlocked. The freed mind is limitless and in terms of successes, accomplishments, and achievements, the sky is even lower in exploitation. The mind can imprison or liberate the individual. Be watchful and fully aware of the controlling power of the mind.

The Controlling Power of the Mind

The human mind is the "storage" of both negative and positive thoughts. There is a continuous battle going on in the mind. Failure or success begins in the mind. Indeed, it is the "battleground" for the whole body. The spiritual encounter between Jesus and Satan (Matt. 4 and Luke 4) though depicted to have taken place in the wilderness, as a matter of fact, it was more of "mind-battle" as good and evil confronted each other. The victory won by Jesus with the Word of God speaks volumes to the power in the Word and also the unparalleled weapon the Christian is blessed with in times of spiritual warfare. The Apostle Paul though fought physical exchanges of battle, he also had "mind-battle" –Just before dawn Paul urged them all to eat.

> "For the last fourteen days," he said, "you have been in constant suspense and have gone without food- you haven't eaten anything. Now I urge you to take some food. You need it to survive. Not one of you will lose a single hair from his head" (Acts 27:33-34, NIV).

It is therefore not surprising that he exhorted believers in Rome in these words quoted earlier from Romans 12:1-2.

The journey to every victory in your life begins with the mind. As much as environmental factors and conditions affect one's success or failure in life, to a large extent, the final outcome germinates and blossoms in the mind. With hard work of sleepless nights, and uncompromising determination, the student makes excellent grades of "A" and moves to the next level/ladder in academia, and eventually graduates to secure an impressive job of one's choice as a professional to make good money to support one's family. The converse story of failure is equally true.

Throughout this book I will be emphasizing on positive confession, self-determination, hard work, and trust in God based on God's Word, and a life of prayer, to leave behind the "prolonged winter" of failure, negativity, self-pity, sorrow, and "the I cannot do it attitude." Be positive and ever-determined to get over the predicament you are going through now. Phil. 4:13 should be your anchor scriptural verse- "I can do all things through Christ, who strengthens me" (WEB). If it is physical healing, claim it by faith as you look beyond the ordinary and the humanly impossible. Knowing that the price for our physical healing was secured by Jesus' sacrificial death on the cross.

> "He used his servant body to carry our sins to the Cross so we could be rid of sin, free to live the right way. His wounds became your healing" (1 Pt. 2:24, TMB).

Yes, the medical report is not good but God is more than able to heal you. Speak positively to your spirit and believe God for a three hundred and sixty degrees (360 degrees) turn around. Healing in this context is generic and encompasses physical, emotional, and spiritual. Cultivate the habit of speaking life into whatever thing that is dead in your life- health, academics, career, finance, marriage, ministry, family issues, relationships, and others.

The Mind is Now free

When you have unlocked your healing from the "mind closet," freedom, abundance, fruitfulness, prosperity, peace, progress, success, and victory become your portion (Without consultation, plans are frustrated, but with many counselors they succeed – (Prov. 15:22, NASB). The counselors in this context is divine counseling based on the Word of God. If there is any time to renew your mind to achieve greatness, it is now. Dr. Paul Meler asks the question: **"How Important is Renewing Your Mind?** Before providing his answers, Dr. Meler remarks that students who practiced almost daily Scripture meditation for three years or longer were significantly healthier and happier than students who did not meditate on Scripture daily. Also, they were significantly healthier and happier than students who had meditated on Scripture daily for less than three years. Now he provides these answers to the above question:

1. Experiencing the abundant fruit-filled Christian life rather than bitterness, depression, and anxiety is dependent upon a renewing of the mind.

2. Renewing the mind can come from various sources: confrontation from a loving friend, therapy with a Christian counselor, the Holy Spirit's conviction, biblical teaching, and daily meditation on Scripture.

3. Renewing the mind is a continual process needing daily input from God and His Word.

4. Daily meditation on Scripture, with personal application, is the most effective means of obtaining personal joy, peace, and emotional maturity.

5. It generally takes about three years of daily Scripture meditation to produce mental health and happiness that is statistically superior.

6. Group C (characterized by psychological conflict and emotional pain) did not have anyone who regularly meditated on Scripture.

7. Most of the students who daily meditated on Scripture were in Group A (the group with superior mental health, maturity, and happiness) and some were in Group B (normal health and happiness).

Do you struggle with bitterness, anxiety, depression, or other emotional pain? Perhaps you need to meditate on Scriptural truths more and renew your mind in the hope of Jesus Christ. The study showed that renewing your mind daily consistently over a long period time will reap the biggest benefits.

These findings should be of no surprise to us because God promises it to be true in Psalm 1:1-3:

> "Blessed is the man who walks not in the counsel of the wicked, nor stands in the way of sinners, nor sits in the seat of scoffers; but his delight is in the law of the Lord; and on his law he meditates day and night. He is like a tree planted by streams of water that yields its fruit in its season, and its leaf does not wither. In all that he does, he prospers."

CHAPTER 1

The Power Of The Mind

The Mind Controls the Whole Body

Like the anchor of the big ship, the controlling power of the mind over the whole body is unimaginable.

"A person without self-control is like a city with broken-down walls" (Prov. 25:28, NLT).

The mind takes whatever you give it for "data processing." With the term mind power, we usually mean the overall capacity of the mind. It can be expressed in many ways, some of which are listed below:

1. Cognitive Abilities
2. Intelligence
3. Creativity
4. Talents
5. Way of Thinking
6. Consciousness
7. Intuition

Mind power like intelligence, cannot be measured on an absolute scale. It has infinite dimensions. Two people may have great mind power, but it may be impossible to say who is stronger. In some cases, people have superior specific mental abilities, but they lack in other skills. Interesting is the fact that the skills that may be lacking are considered quite common. You may not be able to measure your mind power, but it is evident that you can increase it through practice. Many techniques can help you towards accomplishing this aim. Mastering some of them will improve your everyday living quality. Also, it will make your reality a "bit" more interesting.

For example, imagine how great it would be if you could read a whole book in just 2 hours. Imagine all this knowledge you would be able to absorb. A method like that is undoubtedly a life changer. The good news here is that this is possible and anyone can do it. Motivation and patience is the key. (Source: Brain Evolution System: The Most Powerful Self-Development Technology on Earth").

Negative Thoughts and Failure

Negative thoughts are processed and the end result is evil, and failure. Physical failures occur as a result of mind-set, mentality, and attitude. But the Word of God clearly and emphatically states that you were born according to a divine plan and purpose, and therefore, you cannot fail.

> "For I know the plans I have for you, declares the Lord, plans to prosper you and not to harm you, plans to give you hope and a future" (Jer. 29:15, NIV).

Positive Thoughts and Holistic Healing

You were born with a destiny and until that destiny is accomplished, you cannot die but live to declare the goodness of the Lord.

> "I shall not die, but live, and declare the works of the Lord" (Psalm 118:17, KJV).

Living according to the Word of God is victory. Do not limit your progress by leaning unto your own limited understanding of life.

> "Trust in the Lord with all your heart, And lean not on your own understanding; In all your ways acknowledge Him, And He shall direct your paths" (Prov. 3:5-6, NKJV).

Positive confession and thoughts heal every dead area/aspect of your life miraculously and mysteriously beyond what is written in the books by the professionals and experts. It is not far from your situation; it is just at your doorstep to exercise it. You only have to step out in faith. Just as you do not enter into conversation with a chair to check if it can carry your weight but by faith you sit on it confidently, reach out to hold the helm of Jesus' garment for your instant breakthrough. Your intellectual mind will like to do some "laboratory investigation and analysis" before it embraces this spiritual truth under discussions. Just release your faith for the extraordinary miracle to happen to the extraordinary person like you. Read on hopefully and expectantly.

Physical and Spiritual Failures

The mind is constantly under continued (24/7) attack by Satan as he works with principalities and other demonic forces. Their operations thrive best on spiritual ignorance. Knowledge is power, and lack of knowledge is powerlessness. In Hos.4:6, the Scripture renders no apology to no one and says that **"My People are destroyed due to ignorance."** You must therefore be alert to the things of the spirit.

What are some of the common dreams you constantly have? Do you see dead family members, coffin, people at funeral in red or black/mourn cloth (be contextual here as you interpret because of cultural differences and interpretations of colors; red or black in one culture is different from the interpretation in my own culture) - this is the spirit of premature death on assignment (King Hezekiah was going to die prematurely but when he pleaded with God, the prophet Isaiah came with the good news of 15 more years of extension) - Isa. 38. Spirit of retrogression is on the attack when your dreams send you back to either your village in your home country, primary/elementary/high school/college or former house/work ("menial beginners' job"). These and others connote backwardness/retrogression which impede progress. Spirit of failure is at work when your efforts do not yield maximum fruit/dividends. What others do to make profit/money easily brings you failure/loss. You continue to move in a circle without any forward movement.

You are possibly under spiritual attack when someone known or unknown sleeps with you in your dreams. This means that spiritually you are married to a spirit/ spiritual marriage contracted. Satan tries to get closer to you through dreams to attack you and consequently destroys anything most precious and dear to you. Like any guerrilla warfare, all things being equal, the closer the enemy, the more destructive the damage when the gun is shot.

Spirit of fear attacks and makes you easily fearful about almost everything- fear of failure, fear of the future, fear of death, and others. You develop phobia about almost everything. Some other common spirits that attack us are: anxiety, restlessness, doubt/unbelief/disbelief/, frustration, anger, envy, greed, inferiority or superiority complex, lust, and others. These individual spirits attack at different times but unfortunately, but interestingly, they are "good team players," that work harmoniously to attack a common enemy. Christians must do same on a more positive note and unite to attack the common enemy and his cohorts; and further do exploits to change our own situations and those of others. You must remember that we were born with a purpose and destiny to fulfill. You are a destiny-changer as well as a generational-changer.

Positive Confession Leads to Victory

These spirits try to get hold of you through your mind. But the believer must keep on fighting with the Word of God as exemplified by Jesus until victory is won eventually. I wish to borrow from Betty Miller in her book titled *Positive Affirmations: What the Bible Says About Our Confessions,* to amplify my point of emphasis here.

Betty says that as Christians, our confession should be what we term a "Biblical confession" instead of just a "positive affirmation or confession." We are not talking about confessing our sins here, but rather confessing or acknowledging with our mouth the truths from God's Word. Certainly the Bible tells us to confess our sins, but that is not the only confession we need to make. We are also told to confess or speak out loud the promises of God, in faith, so we can through faith and patience receive them.

> **"That you do not become sluggish, but imitate those who through faith and patience inherit the promises" (Heb. 6:12, NKJV).**

The Bible says confession encourages God's desire to bless us. If we speak positively it will come to pass. The Word of God says in Psalm 50:23 that **"Whoso offereth praise glorifieth me and to him that ordereth his conversation aright will I shew the salvation of God."**

> **"A man's belly shall be satisfied with the fruit of his mouth; and with the increase of his lips shall he be filled. Death and life are in the power of the tongue: and they that love it shall eat the fruit thereof"(Prov. 18:20-21).**

We must not only claim God's Word, but also learn to speak or confess His Word. We must confess our faith in God's Word. Is there any lack in your life? Then hear/read and confess the Word of God into your spirit as below:

> **"My God shall supply all your (my) need according to his riches in glory by Christ Jesus" (Phil. 4:19).**

CHAPTER 2

Potentiality Maximization

Full Utilization of the Mind Power

The human mind is like a sophisticated processing machine with greater efficiency. Failure to use renders it ineffectively valueless, and mal-functional. On the contrary however, it maximizes its full potential when it is put to maximum work by the "operator." The mind in some ways is likened to the body. It does not like any push or disturbance to go the extra mile. The body enjoys to eat, sleep, and have fun. Spiritually, the body opposes to fasting, either short or long term. The more the mind is exercised to the fullest, the greater we maximize our potential. You have an in-built potential and capability to do whatever God puts on your heart as his child to do.

Have you ever thought about the Wright brothers and the invention of airplane? (Accordingly to Wikipedia, Orville and Wilbur Wright were two American brothers, inventors, and aviation pioneers, who are generally credited with inventing, building, and flying the world's first successful airplane. They made the first controlled, sustained flight of a powered, heavier –than air aircraft on December 17, 1903, four miles south of Kitty Hawk, North Carolina. In 1904-1905 the brothers developed their flying machine into the fist practical fixed-wing aircraft. Although not the first to build and fly experimental aircraft, the Wright brothers were the first to invent aircraft controls that made fixed-wing powered flight possible). How on earth can such a huge object carry heavy load and fly in the air? The airplane of today was conceived in the mind by the Wright brothers. Though they are no longer living with us today, their brain child still exists all through life.

Each time I fly my faith in God is renewed and deepened because the whole "theology of aerodynamics" humbles and amazes me. Experts in Physics, Mathematics (geometry), Geography (climatology) continue to put into excellent use what they learned in the classroom to the benefit of humanity- air travelers.

> "But you, Daniel, keep these words secret, and seal the book until the end times. Many will travel everywhere, and knowledge will grow" (Daniel 12:4, GWT).

This prophetic insight received by Daniel, is confirmed, fulfilled, and made possible to a large extent, by the power of the mind in motion.

To talk about the huge ship on the deep blue sea/Atlantic Ocean will not be an exaggeration but too difficult to comprehend by the simple-minded person. This brings to mind my Ordinary Level (O' Level)/High School Physics - that the weight of the volume displaced by the ship is equal to the weight of the ship (Archimedes Principle;

$$\text{Formula:} \frac{\text{Density of Object}}{\text{Weight Density of Fluid}} = \frac{\text{Weight}}{\text{Weight of Displaced Fluid}}$$

"Any object wholly or partially immersed in a fluid, is buoyed up by a force equal to the weight of the fluid displaced by the object. Practically, the Archimedes principle allows the buoyancy of an object partially or wholly immersed in a liquid to be calculated. The downward force on the object is simply its weight."

Education (Informal and Formal) and Intellectuality

The human mind is developed either though formal or informal education. The development of the mind in relation to disease and its treatment, medical science, is another mind-boggling. The whole area of laboratory investigations, diagnosis/prognosis, treatment, and wellness is a mystery, if not a miracle. How the body goes under anesthesia and surgery performed for hours only confirms the first-ever surgery on Adam by God to produce Eve.

> **"So the Lord God caused the man to fall into a deep sleep; and while he was sleeping, he took one of the man's ribs and closed up the place with flesh. Then the Lord God made a woman from the rib he had taken out of the man, and he brought her to the man" (Gen 2:21-22, NIV).**

The wonders of the mind can go on unending. Let us now refresh our minds with how a baby's mind develops and grows through the process of socialization- parents, siblings, other family members, friends, neighbors, the school system, church, social agencies, and the larger community.

The family is the child's first school. The child learns of oneself and others through parental guidance, love, and socialization. The next phase of learning for the child begins, when educators take over with Nursery, Kindergarten, Primary, Elementary, High School, College, Masters/Graduate School, Doctorate, Post-Doctorate Studies, and continued research. Through the above process, the individual's brain develops so much so that if utilized positively and guided by the Word of God, the Bible, this individual becomes like one's creator in every aspect of one's societal and spiritual life. Why? Because God created us in his own image.

> **So God created human beings in his own image. In the image of God, he created them; male and female he created them" (Gen. 1:27, NLT).**

All the attributes of God are literally transferred to this God- person. Scripture tells us that the believers were first called Christians in

Antioch (Acts 11:19-26). Exhibiting the character of God is an integral part of the Christian Life/New Life. The Christian consciously and intentionally chooses to bear fruit that will last eternally.

The mind that rejects God only invites trouble for oneself. The Word of God does not mince words at all and emphatically says that;

> **"...And even as they did not like to retain God in their knowledge, God gave them over to a reprobate mind, to do those things which are not convenient" (Rom. 1:28, KJV).**

The fundamental trouble in our world today is the fact that many have totally rejected God and not just partially. This is scary to the human race of this present generation and the next, if we do not repent. It is seriously detrimental to reject God for any conceivable reason whatsoever. Some reject Him either because they are too intellectual to comprehend the need for God, or too rich to serve Him. There are people more knowledgeable and richer than you and yet, are seriously serving God wholeheartedly in spirit and in truth. It takes a humble heart to serve the creator God. Jesus had it all but he humbled himself to the point of dying on the Cross at Calvary to save you personally.

> **"Think of yourselves the way Christ Jesus thought of himself. He had equal status with God but didn't think so much of himself that he had to cling to the advantages of that status no matter what. Not at all. When the time came, he set aside the privileges of deity and took on the status of a slave, became human! Having become human, he stayed human. It was an incredibly humbling process. He didn't claim special privileges. Instead, he lived a selfless, obedient life and then died a selfless, obedient death — and the worst kind of death at that: a crucifixion. Because of that obedience, God lifted him high and honored him far beyond anyone or anything, ever,**

> so that all created beings in heaven and on earth — even those long ago dead and buried — will bow in worship before this Jesus Christ, and call out in praise that he is the Master of all, to the glorious honor of God the Father" (Phil 2:5-12 TMB).

I am totally dependent on Christ. I mean totally. Because in him I live and move and have my being (Acts 17:28). The ensuing Scripture in Heb. 10:31, King James Version, which keeps resounding a bell of caution to me, is the fact that, **"It is a fearful thing to fall into the hands of the Living God."** The time to renew your mind unto victory is here and now. The fear of God through His Word, enables us to enjoy continued vertical relationship with Him, and consequently empowers us to equally enjoy the horizontal relationship and fellowship ("fellows in the same ship") with one another in the same family, community, church, and country. Individuals, communities, and nations are at war with each other because they themselves are not at peace within and without, and with God. It is as simple as that.

Fellowship with God makes room for another meaningful horizontal fellowship because acts of love, charity, mercy, care for the sick and needy, and concern for one another first and foremost, starts with oneself. This genuine concern will only add to and make our world a better place than we came to meet it.

Sound Mind and the "Beautiful City"

The sound and lovely mind thus becomes a "beautiful city" of progress, prosperity, harmony, sacredness, solemnity, friendship, fellowship, and peace. This "new way" invariably leads to the fullest utilization and maximization of human potentialities and capabilities to "cultivate" and improve our immediate environment proactively. According to Jesus in John 8:32, paraphrased, knowledge is power and can liberate even generations unborn from any form of captivity and limitations of life. Positively applied knowledge sets free.

CHAPTER 3

The Mind Controls The Environment

Afforestation or Desertification is a Choice of the Mind

One individual is ecofriendly and the other is hostile to the environment. One country encourages and promotes re-afforestation to protect the environment and the natural greenery and ecology but another nation cuts off almost all the huge tropical tress for instant money and gratification, which results in desertification and patch land of grassland that serves as a catalyst to bushfires. This is very typical of most African countries. Both choices in question above stem from the mind, both as leadership decision, and the mentality of the people- either to eat one's eggs today or breed more hens for the next generation to enjoy. There is a similar biblical account which is synonymous to the above example. Only a small bowl of soup which had a transient satisfaction consequently robbed Esau of his birthright and inheritance, as the elder and first born to his father Isaac. This is a word of caution for both the author and the reader.

> "Jacob was boiling pottage (lentil stew) one day, when Esau came from the field and was faint [with hunger]. And Esau said to Jacob, I beg of you, let me have some of that red lentil stew to eat, for I am faint and famished! That is why his name was called Edom [red]. Jacob answered, then sell me today your birthright (the rights of a firstborn). Esau said, see here,

> I am at the point of death; what good can this birthright do me? Jacob said, swear to me today [that you are selling it to me]; and he swore to [Jacob] and sold him his birthright. Then Jacob gave Esau bread and stew of lentils, and he ate and drank and rose up and went his way. Thus Esau scorned his birthright as beneath his notice" (Gen. 25:29-34, AMP).

Individuals, Families, and Nations Make a "Mind-Choice"

Choice is crucial in our daily lives. We make choices always as individuals, families, communities, churches/ministries, and nations. Some of these choices are excellent and beneficial, and the converse is also true. This is to say that, some people make bad choices, which they later regret. The young adult is faced with the choice of the school to attend, the course (s) to study, the career to pursue (Engineering, law, medicine, nursing, teaching, or other), the city to live in after graduation, and the company to work with, and finally, the spouse to marry, and the type of family to have. These are all very important, crucial, and critical choices/decisions others have either already made, making, or yet to make. Divine direction becomes indispensable because of Prov. 3: 6, which instructs that, "In all your ways submit to him, and he will make your paths straight."

Marriage and Family

Marriage and family life comes only second to Salvation in Jesus Christ. This choice has a lasting impact on both husband and wife and future children. There is therefore, the need for a prayerful preparation, and never to move by emotions and considerations like beauty, level of education, career, family background, and others. These in themselves are not bad but divine direction should be sought to lead us to them.

Nations

National leaders make choices and decisions every day but I am not analyzing these choices in my book. I leave that to the experts and the reader. However, I commend all leaders who have made excellent and beneficial decisions to meet national aspirations and needs. Other poor-choice nations can learn from others for the benefit of their citizenry. Governments and nations choose to rule by a type of governance, either democratic or undemocratic, and which areas to emphasize on during their tenure of office. It could be health, education, transportation (road, air, or sea), youth development, constitutional reforms, rural/urban development, to revamp agriculture/economy, immigration and security, legal system, or energy. In all these, choices will have to be made to ensure the equitable distribution of the national cake to the citizenry. In context, a choice is a product and matter of the mind. A choice made with God at the center is assured of great success and outcome, despite the accompanying challenges. In Genesis 13 Abram made an all-time God-driven decision and experienced great success.

> "Finally Abram said to Lot, "Let's not allow this conflict to come between us or our herdsmen. After all, we are close relatives! The whole countryside is open to you. Take your choice of any section of the land you want, and we will separate. If you want the land to the left, then I'll take the land on the right. If you prefer the land on the right, then I'll go to the left." Lot took a long look at the fertile plains of the Jordan Valley in the direction of Zoar. The whole area was well watered everywhere, like the garden of the Lord or the beautiful land of Egypt. (This was before the Lord destroyed Sodom and Gomorrah.) Lot chose for himself the whole Jordan Valley to the east of them. He went there with his flocks and servants and parted company with his uncle Abram. So Abram settled

in the land of Canaan, and Lot moved his tents to a place near Sodom and settled among the cities of the plain" (Gen 13:8-13, NLT).

The Story/Plight of Poor and Rich Nations

At this juncture I wish to quote excerpts from an article posted by Mr. Augustine Boahen, General Secretary, Council of Brong Ahafo Associations of North America (COBAANA), at the General Forum on June 10, 2016, which incidentally had an Unknown Author. These points support my heart cry about developing and developed nations. Read below for more insight into the problems at stake:

The difference between the poor and rich nations is not the age of the nation. This can be demonstrated by countries like India and Egypt, which are more than 2000 years old and are still poor countries.

On the other hand, Canada, Australia, and New Zealand, which 150 years back were insignificant, today are developed countries.

The difference between the poor and rich nation does not also depend on the available natural resources. Japan has limited territory, 80% mountainous, unsuitable for agriculture or farming, but is the second in world's economy. The country is like an immense floating factory importing raw materials from the whole world and exporting manufactured products.

A second example is Switzerland. It does not grow cocoa but produces the best chocolates in the world. In her small territory she rears animals and cultivates the land only for four months in a year, nevertheless manufactures the best milk products. A small country which is an image of security, which has made it the strongest world bank.

Executives from rich countries who interact with their counterparts from poor countries show no significant intellectual differences.

The racial or color factors also do not evince importance: migrants heavy in laziness in their country of origin are forcefully productive in rich foreign countries.

Why then is the difference? The difference is the attitude of the people moulded for many years by education and culture. When we analyze the conduct of the people from the rich and developed countries, it is observed that a majority abide by the following principle of life:

Basic Principles of Ethics
1. Integrity
2. Responsibility
3. The respect for laws and regulations
4. The respect form majority of citizens by right
5. The love for work
6. The effort to save and invest
7. The will to be productive
8. Punctuality

In the poor countries a small minority follow these basic principles in their daily life.

We are not poor because we lack natural resources or because nature was cruel towards us. We are poor because we lack attitude. We lack the will to follow and teach these principles that are working for the rich and developed societies.

We are in this state because we want to take undue advantage over everything and everyone. We are in this state because we see something done wrong and condone it "let it be." We should have a spirited memory and attitude of caring only then will we be able to change our present state.

Another article posted by Paddymore on the same forum on the same day, June 10, 2016, read: "The Liberian president, Ellen Johnson, said something recently that **"Africa is not poor but poorly managed."**

I personally agree with the issues raised and discussed above. Developing countries, especially, Africa should wake up from our long sleep and put our respective houses/countries in order to reap the full benefits of hard work, patriotism, and nationalism. Corruption (at both high and low places), greed, selfishness, laziness, apathy, shoddy work at some levels, and disrespect for time ("African Punctuality") are but just few of the African "epidemic"/endemic." The reader is encouraged to read my other book titled "African Punctuality": Time is Divine And Of The Greatest Essence to know more about the African situation. What I have mentioned above is just the tip of the iceberg.

For spiritual growth and closer walk with the Lord, the Christian makes a daily choice to give attention to the Word, studies and training, prayer, fasting, witnessing and others. The twenty hours a day has always been so, but prudent choice, excellent time management and utilization make the different between the ant and friends.

> **"You lazy fool, look at an ant. Watch it closely; let it teach you a thing or two. Nobody has to tell it what to do. All summer it stores up food; at harvest it stockpiles provisions. So how long are you going to laze around doing nothing? How long before you get out of bed?" (Prov. 6:6, TMB).**

It is important to note that, intelligent and God-driven choices yield maximum productivity, sustainability, and empirical progress.

Professionals Take Over With Best Choices

In relation to the five basic needs of life (oxygen/air, water, food, shelter/sleep, and clothing), regular choices must be made to ensure judicious distribution to all, for human survival - What to spend?

How to spend it? When to spend it, and who to spend on, and why? These are critical questions for consideration before making an informed choice and decision. It is sad to remark that in certain countries only 10% of the population monopolizes 90% of the available resources and the 90% of the population share the meager 10% of the resources. I hope I am not confusing the reader with this simple arithmetic.

To be able to make reasonable and informed decisions, one must consult the professionals in the respective fields. For example, the architect's professional advise on housing is required to decide on what type of building is suitable to the individual's needs and preferences. Architecture (shelter) has been part of human existence since ancient times to the present. The agriculturists and nutritionists (food) help to address our food and dietary needs. Dr. Maxwell Nartey, Founder and President of Symptometry, and the American School of Symptometry says, **"What we eat or do not eat make us sick. Furthermore, he adds that whatever we eat must be in moderation."**

We daily choose what to wear according to the prevailing environmental condition. A cold winter weather demands heavy clothing and hot/warm summer demands light clothing. The type of clothing is dependent on the environment as exemplified above. We all sometimes take things for granted on daily basis, and therefore, overlook some very important needs in life. The air we breathe is a classic example. Tough supplied freely by God, we inhale oxygen freely for survival, and alternatively exhale carbon dioxide which is beneficial to the growth in plants.

Clean And Healthy Water Is Good Medicine For The Human Body

1. Drinking water helps maintain the balance of body fluids: Your body is composed of about 60% water. The functions of these bodily fluids include digestion, absorption, circulation, creation of saliva, transportation of nutrients, and maintenance of body temperature. Through the posterior pituitary gland, your brain communicates with your kidneys and tells it how much water to excrete as urine or hold onto for reserves, says Guest, who is also an adjunct professor of medicine at Stratford University.

2. Water can help control calories: For years, dieters have been drinking lots of water as a weight loss strategy. While water does not have any magical effect on weight loss, substituting it for higher calorie beverages can certainly help. "What works with weight loss is if you choose water or a non-calorie beverage over a calorie beverage and/or eat a diet higher in water, rich foods that are healthier, more filling, and help you trim calorie intake," says Penn State researcher Barbara Rolls, PhD., author of *The Volumetrics Weight Control Plan*.

Food with high water content tends to look larger, its higher volume requires more chewing, and it is absorbed more slowly by the body, which helps you feel full. Water-rich foods include fruits, vegetables, broth-based soups, oatmeal, and beans.

3. Water helps energize muscles: Cells that don't maintain their balance of fluids and electrolytes shrivel, which can result in muscle fatigue. "When muscle cells don't have adequate fluids, they don't work as well and performance can suffer," says Guest. Drinking enough fluids is important when exercising. Follow the American College of Sports Medicine guidelines for fluid intake before and during physical activity. These guidelines recommend that people drink about 17 ounces of fluid about two hours before exercise. During exercise, they recommended that people start drinking fluids early, and drink them at regular intervals to replace fluids lost by sweating.

4. Water helps keep skin looking good: Your skin contains plenty of water, and functions as a protective barrier to prevent excess fluid loss. But don't expect over-hydration to erase wrinkles or fine lines, says Atlanta dermatologist Kenneth Ellner, MD. "Dehydration makes your skin look more dry and wrinkled, which can be improved with proper hydration," he says. "But once you are adequately hydrated, the kidneys take over and excrete excess fluids." You can also help "lock" moisture into your skin by using moisturizer, which creates a physical barrier to keep moisture in.

5. Water helps your kidneys: Body fluids transport waste products in and out of cells. The main toxin in the body is blood urea nitrogen, a water-soluble waste that is able to pass through the kidneys to be excreted in the urine, explains Guest. "Your kidneys do an amazing job of cleansing and ridding your body of toxins as far as your intake of fluids is adequate," he says. When you are getting enough fluids, urine flows freely, is light in color, and odor increases because the kidneys trap extra fluid for bodily functions. If you chronically drink too little, you may be at higher risk for kidney stones, especially in warm climates, Guest warns.

6. Water helps maintain normal bowel function: Adequate hydration keeps things flowing along your gastrointestinal tract and prevents constipation. When you don't get enough fluid, the colon pulls water from stools to maintain hydration-and the result is constipation. "Adequate fluid and fiber is the perfect combination, because the fluid pumps up the fiber and acts like a broom to keep your bowel functioning properly," says Koelemay.

Five Tips to Help you Drink More

If you think you need to be drinking more, here are some tips to increase your fluid intake and reap the benefits of water:

1. Have a Beverage With Every Snack and Meal.

2. Choose beverages you enjoy. You're likely to drink more liquids if you like the way they taste.

3. Eat more fruits and vegetables. Their high water content will add to your hydration. About 20% of our fluid intake comes from foods.

4. Keep at least bottle of water with you in your car, at your desk or in your bag. Ensure you always have access to water.

5. Choose beverages that meet your individual needs. If you're watching calories, go for non-calorie beverages or water.

(Source: www.m.webmd.com.diet/features/6-reasons -to- drink-water).

Clean water saves the lives of individuals, families, and nations huge sums of money because the money not spent on the treatment of water-borne diseases schistosomiasis (or bilharzia), cholera, and others, is money saved to meet the financial challenges of tomorrow in the form of astronomical and mounting school fees, medical bills, and utilities. Trained experts, "water engineers" or "hydraulic engineers" offer us the needed help with water treatment. It is unbelievable to remark that certain communities elsewhere drink "dirty water" (unpurified and untreatable water) in the 21st century. In the meantime, public education can be of tremendous help. For example, such dirty water can be treated by boiling and sieving before human consumption. This confirms my book title- Renewing Your Mind Unto Victory. Victory here means overcoming preventable water-borne diseases like cholera, which is rampant in some countries regardless the seeming advancement and discoveries made in medical science and technology.

There are many areas of the world where humans do not have access to sufficient potable water or rely on water sources that are contaminated with toxins, suspended solids, pathogens, or diseases vectors. Drinking water, also known as potable water or improved drinking water, is water safe enough for drinking and food preparation. Globally, in 2012, 89% of people had access to water suitable for drinking. Nearly 4 billion had access to tap water while another 2.3 billion had access to wells or public taps (Source: Drinking Water-Wikipedia, the free encyclopedia: Wikipedia>wiki> Drinking –water).

Before concluding this section, I wish to quote Scripture verses to support the importance of water and God's divine purpose for supplying it to humankind.

> "We must all die; we are like water spilled on the ground, which cannot be gathered up" - 2 Sam. 14:14.

> "You visit the earth and water it, you greatly enrich it, the river of God is full of water; you provide the people with, for so you have prepared it" (Psalm 65:9).

> "Like cold water to a thirsty soul, so is good news from a far country"(Prov. 25:25).

> "Those who walk righteously and speak uprightly, who despise the grain of oppression, who wave away a bribe instead of accepting, who stop their ears from hearing of bloodshed and shut their eyes from looking on evil, they will live on the heights; their refuge will be the fortresses of rocks; their food will be supplied, their water assured' (Isa. 33:15-16).

> "For my people have committed two evils: they have forsaken me, the fountain of living water, and dug out cisterns for themselves, cracked cisterns that can hold no water" (Jer. 2:13).

> "But let justice roll on like a river, righteous like a never-failing stream" (Amos 5:24).

Conclusion

Divine will-power empowers the individual to have dominion over the immediate environment. Differently put, the mind is to positively control the environment to one's advantage through well-informed, God-centered choices/decisions, and never meant to be the opposite way, which is the order of the day.

> **"God bless them and said to them, Be fruitful and increase in number; fill the earth and subdue it. Rule over the fish in the sea and the birds in the sky and over every living creature that moves on the ground" (Gen.1:28, NIV).**

Unfortunately, despite all the blessings of God, mankind still appears to be totally engulfed and immersed in ignorance, arrogance, diseases, poverty, disbelief, self-centeredness, greed, pride, suspicion, and the fear of the unknown. Desertification and its accompanying problems of famine, rampant yearly bushfires, and the like, must cease but the cessation is of the mind. This leads us to another interesting discussion in the next chapter.

CHAPTER 4

Nations Are Developed By Brains, Not Natural Resources

Abundant Natural Resources

Even though the book emphasizes on the controlling power of the mind, I refer to this chapter as the "Brain Development Chapter." I will start the discussion with the statement that "brains develop a nation and not natural resources necessarily." The reader is to wear one's "academic hat" to follow the basic argument put forward. Nation "A" has abundance of natural resources like cocoa, timber, minerals, oil, and others, but it is still poor due to corruption in both high and low places, greed, mismanagement, poor supervision, the citizenry's unethical attitude towards work; lateness, low productivity, and lackadaisical attitude towards government-based jobs and employment (one of the "legacies" of the colonial master bequeathed to us through the system of education, as well as the cultural mentality of the people and here, specifically, some African countries). These are all matters and decisions/choices of the mind. The mind is the focal point in all of these apathetic behaviors.

Another country "B" has developed relatively her best brains over the years through the educational system, which is relevant to the job market economy, through practical training during internships. Some of the human resource problems enumerated under nation "A" above, are strictly under control, and very minimal indiscipline, and poor work ethics, which invariably promote and boost productivity, and the national income (GDP-Gross Domestic Product); and foreign exchange to create more jobs to absorb the yearly large size of young graduates from the universities and other tertiary institutions. The acquisition of job after graduation justifies the need for education and serves as an impetus to campaign for more educational funding, scholarships, and research grants in these developed nations.

Excellent Human Resources

With the many advantages that come with excellent human resources, I do not in any way suggest that on its own, it can sustain the economy. Differently expressed, the human resources must combine effectively with the abundant natural resources for meaningful development and sustainability. The excellent labor force ensures an all-year round production and job maintenance, and relatively low loss of jobs, and unemployment. The story is the very opposite with many of the countries with abundant natural resources like cocoa, minerals (gold, bauxite, manganese, diamond, and oil). Most developing countries in Africa and elsewhere, that are rich in natural resources are still poor as discussed earlier in chapter three. What a paradox? But it is evidently factual. The poverty emanates from the mind and not the natural resources per se.

The Brain Takes the Lead

The controlling power of the mind takes the lead to train the best brains in the various schools and universities. The decision to embark on a particular program and not the other, or revise the existing one, is the choice of the mind. The brain takes the lead either individually or collectively in any decision to go for war or not. Great and major world wars started in the minds of leaders in the conference rooms or in parliament, where many best brains and minds gave the final approval to the war budget.

The Word of God says that a man and of course, a woman, without self-control is as defenseless as a city with broken down walls – Prov. 25:28. The decision to either leave old friends, make new friends, maintain existing relationships, or to let go of a past hurt/wound, is a matter of choice which is also of the mind. Let us allow the spirit of God (Gen, 1:1, 1 Corn. 3:17, John 14:26, and John 15:26) to control our "engine room"- mind/brain, which is the focal point/melting point of all ideas and decisions, good or evil. The mind, among others, is the "battleground" of the human body. The source of our disgrace or honor is the mind. Mind-control thus becomes a daily occurrence we cannot do without. The mind under the submission of the Word of God, and the direction of the Holy Spirit is the greatest gift of life. Helen Keller, an author, says it beautifully in these words **"Toleration is the greatest gift of the mind; it requires the same effort of the brain that it takes to balance oneself on a bicycle."**

Each Benefits From the Other

Just as both hands are needed to wash the body, abundant natural resources and human resources combine to develop the potentials in the individual, family, community, church, and nation. One must not be developed at the expense of the other. Developed and developing countries need each other; each supplements and complements the other. Globalization must promote human dignity, respect, and harmonious living, equitable distribution of resources, and support for one another. The "economic giants" must help the "economic dwarfs" to develop their economies by giving reasonable loans without strings. The time to break the cycle of poverty is now, it a decision, choice, and mind-matter.

To Achieve Holistic Development

The catch word here is "holistic." Local communities and the international community/global village must reap the full benefits of globalization; increase economic growth, and generate a wider range of products and services. Supporters of globalization argue that the benefits of a more interdependent global economy outweigh the drawbacks. Economies that are developing globally have more economic growth than established economies, demonstrating globalization's benefits for developing regions. Foreign exchange allows more products and services to be available, while also lowering costs, because of specialization. The primary argument in favor of globalization as a value-added international trend calls for critical examination by all.

Other obvious benefits of globalization are: increased wealth-one pro-globalization argument involves how, based on per capita Gross Domestic Product (GDP) growth rates, developing countries become wealthier. In the 1960s, non-globalized economies grew at an annual rate of 1.4%, while globalized economies grew at 4.7%. A second argument in favor of globalization involves the rise of political philosophies, based on the assumption that free markets follow a natural trajectory towards democratic and capitalistic philosophies. Better quality of life is the next. Although there is opposition to globalization from some religious and social activists, proponents argue that the widespread availability of global goods, services, and ideas positively impacts the lifestyle of citizens. Some of the different areas where advocates claim globalization benefits individuals include:

1. Better access to external financing some as car and home loans.

2. More opportunities for international travel and tourism.

3. More opportunities to work abroad due to liberal immigrant laws and foreign worker programs.

4. Greater consumption of worldwide entertainment including music, sports, fads and pop culture.

5. The rapid spread of consumer products (e.g. food, clothing brands) to other countries.

The final argument supporting globalization's benefits focusses on how globalization leads to the increased availability of diverse products, services, and technology. Through pooling knowledge and exchanging more goods and services, domestic economies expand and benefit from technological and medical developments. This increase in variety, even in basic goods, allows someone in Spain to drink Italian wine and eat French cheese while typing on a Chinese keyboard. Global exchange can allow the best of all worlds through specialization and maximizing various comparative advantage that involve quality or efficiency.

Source:https://www.boundless.com/management/textbook/boundless/ management/textbook/globalization-and-business-14/globalization-101/ benefits-of-globalization -470-3958/.

CHAPTER 5

Divine Power Is Supreme

The Brain is Central to Development

The earlier chapters have already established the fact that the brain is central to human development. Though the human brain is hidden, it has such a great power of influence either positively or negatively. Behind the tall magnificent buildings in downtown Chicago, are as a result of best brains at work on the drawing board, and also true for the complex network of roads, air travel, and large ships on the deep blue sea. These brains spend quality time to sit at the feet of professionals in schools to develop in order to impact lives in their respective fields. From the days of Aristotle, Plato, and Archimedes, nations and countries have taken time to train best minds. The fast-moving development in science, technology, and communication is just amazing. Universities have engaged best brains in continued research.

I wrote this book from the University of Chicago Regenstein library and I was always challenged by how young students work hard day in and day out to excel in their respective disciplines of study. In the University Bus 171, I would see promising young law students carrying their many big books as they board. Campus life depicts the seriousness at which most students assiduously discipline themselves to train their minds for the competitive job market in the US and globally. The acquisition of the best job starts from the mind/brain. Individuals go the extra mile to be ready for the awaiting-interviews, orientation, and employment out there. There is a great lesson developing nations can learn from relatively developed countries like the US.

The Pen is Mightier Than the Sword

To talk about the pen is to talk about the mind. The pen is the product of the mind. In other words, through the development of the brain, the art of writing moved from papyrus (the word papyrus refers to a thick type of paper made from the pith of the papyrus plant tree age) to scrolls, fountain pen and ink era, then ball-point pens, and now to laptops, tablets, and other forms of writing to keep records and information. Other professionals use special codes, which are totally different to communicate. The idea to go for any war first started in the mind, and then by a written paper/document to parliament for either approval or disapproval. A stroke of the pen can either start or end a war. "The pen is mightier than the sword" is metonymic adage indicating that communication, or in some interpretations, administrative press, is more effective tool than direct violence." The sentence (if not the idea, which had been expressed in various earlier forms) was coined by English author Edward Bulwer-Lytton in 1839 for his play Richelleu, Or the Conspiracy. In sum, it means that writing is more effective than military power or violence.

What The Brain Can See and Do

Great Artists and designers add to the beauty of creation and our immediate environment. Their minds see what the ordinary eye cannot see. The seeing power leads them to the doing power. I met a long –time brother, Rexford in New York on April 22, 2016, and I was amazed by some of the things he shared with me about his creative ability and acumen. Looking at the furniture in the sitting room, he described into detail creative skills too difficult for me to understand. The power of the brain is amplified by this simple example from Rexford. **"Perceiving an idea is God-given, translating the idea on the drawing board by way of designing, is creative power, and implementing/concretizing it practically is "divine beauty" in excellence. Indeed, the brain can see and do beyond the ordinary."**

Renewal and Transformation (Rom. 12:1-2)

According to the Scriptures, Apostle Paul makes a passionate appeal to all Christians to live a holy life that is acceptable to God, as we engage in the process of renewing our mind.

> **"I beseech you therefore, brethren, by the mercies of God, that ye present your bodies, a living sacrifice, holy, acceptable unto God, which is your reasonable service. And be not conformed to this world: but be ye transformed by the renewing of your mind, that ye may prove what is that good, and acceptable, and prefect, will of God."**

The word "therefore" in the Scripture above, invites the reader to go back to read Romans Chapter 11.

The old nature/life must give way to a new way of living. The power to renew or transform comes from the mind. This comes to buttress my earlier discussion on the controlling power of the mind. To change or not change, is from the mind. To live a reformed life, is the mind touched by the Holy Spirit. To settle scores with one another is possible and easy only when the mind gives the approval. Paul further exhorts in Rom. 12:21, and says that, **"Do not be overcome by evil, but overcome evil with good."**

The reformed mind is peaceful, and the peaceful mind is proactive and progressive. All things being equal, much is achieved during peace time than war time. Greater discoveries and inventions are locked up in the mind that is full of hatred, hostility, greed, envy, selfishness, corruption, bike-biting, jealousy, egocentrism, pride, know it all, disrespect, self-conceit, restlessness, and recklessness. These attitudes hinder progress, promotion, projection, productivity, and proactivity. The individual, family, community, church, or nation does not look far like the ostrich, but is not aware, for the simple reason that it buries its head and dreams in the heavy desert sand. Nations with short-sighted developmental plans fall into this category. The road under construction is too narrow to accommodate the teeming/heavy traffic. And before the road is commissioned, the first phase of the same project already needs repairs. This is the time for holistic mind renewal and transformation.

On the Road to Victory

The road to victory starts with the mind and it is now. Victory is relative and peculiar to the individual. Whatever challenges you, confront it now, because it is surmountable through mind development. The student passes the examination before it starts. This comes through hard work of studies and sleepless nights. The mind is able to possess or dispossess, lock or unlock, arm or disarm, do or undo, empower or be empowered, engage or disengage, and love and be loved. The road to victory starts with the fruit of the spirit as enumerated in this Scripture below.

> **"But the Holy Spirit produces this kind of fruit in our lives: love, joy, peace, patience, kindness, goodness, faithfulness, gentleness, and self-control. There is no law against these things" (Gal. 5:22-23, NLT).**

CONCLUSION

Self-Development ("At the Library Now")

Self-development is a choice and a conscious decision. In the area of academics, the student spends hours unending at the library- researching, reading, and writing to be able to turn in an excellent paper at the end of the semester. I wrote this book from the University of Chicago Regenstein library. I am therefore speaking from concrete lived experience. Spiritual self-development comes through a consistent and disciplined life of quiet/devotional time with the Lord in prayer, study of the Word, witnessing, holy living, and continued hunger for the Lord. Others choose to develop their muscle at the gymnasium which is good for healthy living among others. As discussed earlier in the book, self-development is personal, national, and international. It is a choice, a decision, and a "mind-business."

Informal and Formal, Wisdom and Intellect; The Two in Conversation

Through parental and family love and support, we develop social cohesion as we bond with others at home and in the community. The family thus becomes the first school of the child before the local community joins in to raise this child. This is the genesis of the popular adage that it takes a whole village to raise a child. The statement is very much true. In retrospect, I could relate to it while growing up in Ghana as a young person. The basic meaning is that, child-upbringing is a communal/societal effort. The proverb leverages the cultural context and belief that it takes an entire community to raise a child. A child has the best ability to become a healthy adult if the entire community takes an active role in contributing to the raising of the child. Notwithstanding the benefits of the proverb, the story is a bit different in the 21st century in many communities in Africa due to formal education, modernity, individual human rights, child abuse advocacy, parental influence, and others. For sure, the informal lays down the foundation for formal education through socialization when the child learns about self, and the other, and the need to be of help to the needy, and also be able to receive help from others when needed. The Word of God throws more light on this very point.

> "The fear of the Lord is the beginning of wisdom and the knowledge of the Holy One is understanding" (Prov. 9:10).

Sir Thomas Browne, an English physician, writer and theologian also says, **"But how shall we expect charity towards others, when we are uncharitable to ourselves? Charity begins at home, is the voice of the world"**- Sir Thomas Browne, 1642. It was also said by other famous writers and theologians: **"Charity should begin at himself."**- John Wycliffe, 1383. **"Charity begins at home, and justice begins next door."**- Charles Dickens, 1844.

Best Brains Develop Through Education

Much has been said to establish the unparalleled influence of both informal and formal education in the development of the human brain for advancement. Parental and family support nurtures the child to a mature and well-informed adult. The progressive life of many is traceable to their childhood training, and parental care, and family life. The family is the "first school" of the child. Other socializing agents like the close neighborhood/environment, societal norms and values, and the church help shape the individual.

A life of spirituality through consistent family devotion and church attendance is indispensable for a fruitful adult life. The Word of God emphatically states that the fear of God is beginning of wisdom- Prov. 9:10. I can personally attest to the truthfulness of the above quote. In this age of fast-knowledge acquisition as foretold by Prophet Daniel, the temptation to ignore God is real and very high.

> **"But you, Daniel, keep this prophecy a secret; seal up the book until the time of the end, when many will rush here and there, and knowledge will increase" (Dan.12:4, NLT).**

Dear reader, you are humbly encouraged to give God the first place in your life in whatever you lay your hands on to do in this fast-changing and unpredictable world of today.

It is pertinent to understand that, abundant natural resources do not necessarily guarantee holistic development. The fear of God and its accompanying friends; wisdom, and brain development through formal and informal education, produce the needed human resources/technocrats for the 21st century. Personal best brain development comes with countless benefits to the individual, family, community, church, and the nation. At the apex of all forms of development is the supremacy of spiritual development. It is the glory of all forms of developments that can connect, shape, refine, define, and redefine. Consequently, the glory of God crowns and envelopes the individual with any needed glory and honor. I call it holistic development for a meaningful, reformed, and transformed life to the glory of God.

Apostle Paul once again reminds the us that we are all accountable to God as parents, children, husbands, wives, sisters, brothers, and friends to each other. The minister is equally accountable to God for his personal life, and those of his flocks, on how best they were fed or not fed spiritually.

"For we must all appear before the judgment seat of Christ, so that each of us may receive what is due us for the things done while in the body, whether good or bad" (2 Cor. 5:10, NIV).

In conclusion, a Negro Spiritual by James Weldon Johnson titled *Lift Every Voice and Sing* is produced below for the readers' final reflection as I draw the "final curtain" on the ideas expressed and discussed in this book.

Lift every voice and sing.

Till earth and heaven ring.

Ring with the harm-o-nies of Liberty:

Let our rejoicing rise.

High as the lit'ning skies.

Let it resound loud as the rolling sea.

Sing a song full of the faith that the dark past has taught us.

Sing a song full of the hope that the present has brought us;

Facing the rising sun of our new day begun.

Let us march on till Victory is won.

PRAYER OF SALVATION

Acceptance, Rededication, Recommitment, And Refire

Prayer to Accept Jesus Christ as Lord and Savior (ABCD of Salvation)

A—Admit in humility that you are a sinner (Romans 3:23).

B—Believe on the Lord Jesus Christ, and thou shall be saved, and thy house (Acts 16:31).

C—Confess with your mouth the Lord Jesus and believe in your heart that God has raised him from the dead, you will be saved (Rom. 10:9).

D—Dedicate your body to Christ henceforth (Rom 12:1).

Repeat The Prayer After Me:
Lord Jesus, I have heard your word today. I admit that I am a sinner. I confess to you all my sins, known and unknown. Forgive me because I have greatly sinned against you. I accept you as my personal Lord and Savior. Come into my heart; take full control of my life. I hand over the key of my life to you. Take me and make me thy own henceforth. Amen!

If you prayed and believed the prayer, then John 1:12 is for you.

> "...But as many as received him, to them gave he power to become the sons of God, even to them that believe on his name."

REDEDICATION/RECOMMITMENT

"Revive Me, O Lord" (Psalm 119:156)

Please offer This Prayer of Rededication to The Lord:

"Revive Me, O Lord" (Ps. 119:156).

"Restore unto me the joy of your salvation, and grant me a willing spirit, to sustain me" (Ps. 51:12).

"Now the Lord is the Spirit, and where the Spirit of the Lord is, there is freedom" (2 Cor. 3:17).

Prayer By Author For Readers:

Gracious and everlasting God, through the inspiration and power of the Holy Spirit, I pray with the reader right now. Please, Lord, rekindle the individual's spirit with your love and peace, and rejuvenate your child and restore your illumination and enlightenment to the yearning soul. In Jesus' Name. Amen!

FOR ALL "ON FIRE" BRETHREN

Retreat! Retire! And Refire!e!

Prayer:

Come, Holy Spirit, to reenergize me for service!

Let me experience another Pentecost,

A new personal Pentecost in my life!

I receive the new Pentecost fire by faith! In Jesus' Name. Amen!

RECOMMENDED BOOKS

For Further Professional And Spiritual Development

1. *Integral Pastoral Care in Ghana: Proposals for Healing in the Asante Context* by Gabriel Amoateng-Boahen.
2. *The "Culture of Silence" Contributes to Perpetuating Domestic Violence: A Case Study of Family Life in the Brong Ahafo Region of Ghana* by Gabriel Amoateng-Boahen.
3. *Spiritual Mentorship for Pastors and Church Leaders Today* by Gabriel Amoateng-Boahen.
4. *My Ministry is Where My Misery Was* by Gabriel Amoateng- Boahen.
5. *Pastoral Care and Holistic Ministry* by Gabriel Amoateng-Boahen.
6. *The Controlling Power Of The Mind: Renewing Your Mind Unto Victory* by Gabriel Amoateng-Boahen.
7. *African Punctuality: Time Is Divine And Of The Greatest Essence* by Gabriel Amoateng-Boahen.
8. *Testimonies Today Tributes Tomorrow* by Gabriel Amoateng- Boahen.
9. *Spiritual Labour Room: Travailing Prayer* by Veronica Amoateng Antwi.
10. *Guarding and Protecting Your Prophetic Word* by Daniel Amoateng.
11. *Dreams and Their Interpretations* by Daniel & Brian Amoateng.
12. *From Impossibilities to Possibilities* by Daniel Amoateng.
13. *500 Wise Words and Life Lessons* by Daniel Amoateng.
14. *Daily Prophetic Declarations* by Daniel Amoateng.
15. *Exposing Dream Killers* by Daniel Amoateng.
16. *Why Was I Born?* by Daniel Amoateng.

17. *Favour* by Brian Amoateng.
18. *100 Wisdom Tablets* by Brian Amoateng.
19. *Hindrances to Prayer* by Brian Amoateng.
20. *Five Mistakes to Avoid in Life* by Brian Amoateng.
21. *You Can Recover From a Fall* by Brian Amoateng.
22. *Walking in the Favour of God* by Brian Amoateng.
23. *Dreams and Their Interpretations* by Brian Amoateng.
24. *Favor, Your key to Lasting Success* by Brian Amoateng.
25. *Answers God Gives When We Pray* by Brian Amoateng.
26. *Keys to Effective Travelling Ministry* by Brian Amoateng.
27. *The Wonders of Speaking in Tongues* by Mark Amoateng.
28. *How to Receive from God* by Mark Amoateng.
29. *The Law of Seed by* Sampson Amoateng.
30. *Possessing the Kingdom* by Jesse Sackey.
31. *Understanding the Divine Timing of God* by Victor Owusu-Teng.
32. *Understanding Your Divine Calling & Purpose by* Victor Owusu-Teng.
33. *Mission–Minded Skits* by Cynthia Miller.
34. *Mission-Minded Skits* by Cynthia Miller.
35. *Practical Psychology for Pastors* by William R. Miller.
36. *Called to Care: A Christian Theology of Nursing* by Arlene B. Miller.
37. *Restoring Fallen Pastors* by Eric Reed.
38. *Beyond Suffering* by Joni Eareckson Tada.
39. *Pastoral: An Essential Guide* by John Patton.
40. *Prayer: The 30 Most Powerful* by John Bernthal.
41. *The Strategically Small Church* by Brandon O'Brien.
42. *Leadership: Be Humble, Stay Hungry* by Brad Lomenick.
43. *Personal Identity in Theological Perspective* by Richard Lints.
44. *Dangerous Calling: Confronting the Unique* by Paul David Tripp.

Recommended Books For Further Professional And Spiritual Development

45. 48. *In the Name of Jesus Reflections* by Henri J. M. Nouwen.
46. *The Emotionally Healthy Leader: How to Leader* by Peter Scazzero.
47. *Pastoral Care in Context: An Introduction to Pastoral Care* by John Patton.
48. *Being a Pastor: Understanding Our calling and Work* by Derek J. Prime.
49. *Ministerial Ethics: Moral Formation for Church Leaders* by Joe E. Trull.
50. *Fivefold Ministry Made practical: How to Release Apostles, Prophets, Evangelists, Pastors, and Teachers to Equip Today's Church* by Ron Myer.
51. *The Right One: How to Successfully Date and Marry the Right Person* by Jimmy Evans and Frank Martin.
52. *Is God Calling Me?: Answering the Question Every Leader Believer Asks* by Jeff Lorg.
53. *Brothers, We Are Not Professionals: A Plea to Pastors for Radical Ministry* by John Piper.
54. *Be Thou Prepared: Equipping the Church for Persecution and Times of Trouble* by Carl Gallups.
55. *Practical Wisdom for Pastors: Words of Encouragement and Counsel for a Lifetime* by Curtis C. Thomas.
56. *Mentoring Leaders: Wisdom for Developing Character, Calling, and Competency* by Carson Pue.
57. *Preaching: Communicating Faith in an Era of Skepticism* by Timothy Keller.
58. *The Wounded Healer: Ministry in Contemporary Society* by Henri J.M. Nouwen.
59. *Pastoral Bearings: Lived Religion and Pastoral Theology* by Leonard Hammel.
60. *Professional Spiritual and Pastoral Care: A Practical Clergy and Chaplains' Handbook.*

BLURB

According to James N. Watkins, "**a river is able to cut through a rock not because it is powerful, but because of its persistency.**" The persistent brain is a great asset for human and societal development.

This book unearths what the best brain can do when subjected under the authority of God's Word, and through the inspiration and leading of the Holy Spirit. It has a hidden revelation about the mind and so the author asks the question; what is the wealthiest place in the world in relation to the mind? According to Dr. Myles Munroe, it is the cemetery-buried here were dreams and visions that were never fulfilled.

The author lifts the "banner" of the best brain high, and says that, abundant natural resources do not necessarily develop a nation, but best brains. The controlling power of the mind is unimaginable. The time to renew your mind unto victory is NOW!

AUTHOR'S PROFILE

Dr. Gabriel Amoateng-Boahen was born to the Late Opanin Peter Kofi Amoateng (went to be with the Lord in February 1978) and the Late Maame Veronica Yaa Afrah (transitioned to Glory on March 19, 2013, thirty-five years after the death of my father) of Kintampo, Brong Ahafo, Ghana. He started school at the age of seven at the Bodom Presbyterian School and Effia Methodist Primary (near Effiakuma-Takoradi, the Port City). Gabriel returned to Kintampo in 1962 to continue his education at the Baffoe Local Authority and Middle Schools at Kintampo, where he was the Junior Prefect and Senior Prefect respectively (1962-1967; Gabriel's class was the first batch for the new school).

In 1967, Gabriel passed the Common Entrance Examination and gained admission to the Obuasi Secondary Technical School (1967-1972). From 1972-1974, Gabriel successfully completed his Post-Secondary Teacher Training College at Berekum, Brong Ahafo, and was posted to Ahafo Kenyasi II Catholic Primary School. A few weeks later, he was transferred to Ahafo Hwidiem Catholic Primary School, where Gabriel taught from 1974-1984 (part of divine plan unfolding –Jer.29:11).

Gabriel studied privately and passed the Advanced Level Examination and gained admission to pursue his undergraduate studies at the University of Science and Technology (now Kwame Nkrumah University of Science and Technology-KNUST) in Kumasi-Ghana from 1984-1987 and obtained his Bachelor of Arts in Social Sciences (final thesis "Comparative Study of Traditional and Church Marriages in the Brong Ahafo Region: A Case Study of the Hwidiem Traditional Area," UST, Kumasi-Ghana, 1987). From 1987-1989, Gabriel did the mandatory national service at the newly established Community Improvement Unit (CIU) at the Konongo District Office. Gabriel had a "desert experience" from 1990-1991 as he discerned God's plan for his life and also volunteered at the "infant" Maranatha Clinic (now Maranatha Hospital at Kwadaso/Asuoyeboa-Kumasi).

Gabriel was the Diocesan Development Coordinator for the Sunyani Catholic Diocese in 1991 and later became the headmaster for the St. Louis Junior Secondary School at Mbrom-Kumasi from 1992-1994. On May 6, 1995, he became the first-ever headmaster and co-founder of the Maranatha International School (now Maranatha Young Apostles) at Daban Panin-Kumasi. This school was established on sound Christian principles with the motto" Holistic Child Development" to demonstrate the harmonious interplay among hand, head, and heart (hand/body/physical, head/mind/soul/, and heart/the spirit of the human person- 1 Thess.5:23). Prov.9:10 and Prov. 22:6 were our key biblical verses, and both staff and students lived by the precepts of God's Word.

Gabriel arrived in New York on May 31, 2001, to pursue Clinical Pastoral Education (CPE) at the Hospital of Saint Raphael in New Haven, Connecticut, USA, to be trained as a Chaplain, and thereafter proceeded to the Catholic Theological Union (CTU) in Chicago, Illinois, USA, for the Master of Arts in Pastoral Studies (MAPS) from 2002-2004 and the Ecumenical Doctor of Ministry degree from 2004-2007. Gabriel is a Certified Professional Chaplain (Retired) at the University of Chicago Medical Center and also the President and Founder of the Royal Diadem Pastoral Center in Chicago and Kumasi-Ghana.

Gabriel had a personal encounter and relationship with the Lord Jesus Christ on June 6, 1972, and ever since that time, has remained resolute and uncompromising with his Christian faith and has great passion for soul-winning. Gabriel has varied ministerial experiences. He was a member of the Scripture Union, Ghana (especially in the Ahafo and Sunyani areas), from 1974-1984; and he was the church secretary for the Holy Spirit Catholic Church at Ahafo Hwidiem. During that same period, he was the founder and first-ever secretary for the Ahafo Hwidiem Christian Fellowship and was also actively involved in the Council of Churches. Gabriel was the secretary of the first-ever Ghana Catholic School of Evangelization organized by the Germany and Malta teams and hosted by the Metropolitan Archdiocese of Kumasi-Ghana in 1992.

At the Catholic Charismatic Renewal front, Gabriel was a founding member of Mission 2000 (established on November 3, 1991), a Catholic Charismatic Renewal Prayer Group with focus on evangelizing Catholic adults and professionals. He is the current Coordinator of the Charismatic Renewal at Our Lady of Sorrows Basilica at 3121 W. Jackson Boulevard in Chicago, and also a member of the Ghanaian Catholic Charismatic Renewal –North America (G-CCR-NA) Leadership Coordinating Team (LCT) (appointed director for missions in June 2013 at the first-ever National Biennial Convention in Virginia). Gabriel is a founding member of the Ghanaian Catholic Community of Chicago and also the founder and coordinator of the Prayer Conference for the Catholic Community as well as the Christian Leaders for Tomorrow (CL4T) Prayer Conference- youth focused with Daniel 11:32b as its theme verse: "They that know their God shall be strong and do exploits." He is the "marriage counselor" for the local Catholic Community of Chicago and also for some Ghanaians in Chicago.

Gabriel is the Chaplain for the Brong Ahafo Association of Chicago and the keynote speaker at the Council of Brong Ahafo Associations of North America (COBAANA) in 2011; and he is also the Ombudsman for COBAANA. Gabriel has strong ecumenical inclination and is deeply involved in the activities of the Council of Ghanaian Churches in Chicago, where he is the current Vice

President. Gabriel takes a lot of inspiration from Evangelist Dr. Billy Graham. He is Gabriel's "spiritual mentor" and has twice attended the Billy Graham Schools of Evangelism in Cincinnati, Ohio (2002), and Kansas City, Missouri (2004). Gabriel was at the Haggai Institute in Singapore in 2000 for the Advanced Leadership Training for Christian Leaders from Developing Countries.

He is also a bonafide member of these professional associations: National Association of Catholic Chaplains (NACC), Association of Professional Chaplains (APC), Spiritual Direction International (SDI) and others. Gabriel was the representative for the University of Chicago Medical Center at the Kenwood-Hyde Park Interfaith Council (2010 - to May 31, 2015).

On March 27, 1977, Gabriel and Mrs. Agatha Amoateng-Boahen were joined together in holy matrimony at the Holy Spirit Catholic Church at Ahafo Hwidiem. They now live peacefully and happily with their eight children: Mrs. Veronica Amoateng Antwi; Rev. Sampson Amoateng; Rev. Mark Amoateng, MD; Rev. Daniel Amoateng; Rev. Brian Amoateng; Christabel Jessica Amoateng; Davina Amoateng; and Gabriel Amoateng Badu, Jr.

Conferences, Seminars, And Continuous Education

All Pastors and Leaders Conference (APALEC), Stratford Christian Center Church, Chicago, Illinois, USA, 2016.

Ghanaian Catholic Charismatic Renewal –North America (G-CCR-NA), Second Biennial Convention, Bronx, New York, USA, 2015.

All Pastors and Leaders Conference (APALEC), House of Miracles, Medina Estates, Accra-Ghana, 2015.

Ghana Catholic Charismatic Renewal (National Outreach Leaders) Conference, Adom Fie-Kumasi, 2015.

Council of Brong Ahafo Associations of North America (COBAANA) Convention, Bronx, New York, USA, 2014.

Diversity and Inclusion Competency, University of Chicago Medicine, Illinois, USA, Fall 2014.

Ghanaian Catholic Charismatic Renewal –North America (G-CCR-NA), First-Ever Biennial Convention, Falls Church, Virginia, USA, 2013.

Council of Brong Ahafo Associations of North America (COBAANA) Convention, Washington DC, USA, 2013.

All Pastors and Leaders Conference (APALEC), House of Miracles, Medina Estates, Accra-Ghana, 2013.

All Pastors and Leaders Conference (APALEC), Life Community Chapel, Kumasi-Ghana, 2013.

Council of Brong Ahafo Associations of North America (COBAANA) Convention, Columbus, Ohio, USA, 2012.

Council of Brong Ahafo Associations of North America (COBAANA) Convention, Chicago, Illinois, USA, 2011.

All Pastors and Leaders Conference (APALEC), House of Miracles, Medina Estates, Accra-Ghana, 2010.

Council of Brong Ahafo Associations of North America (COBAANA) Convention, Toronto, Canada, 2010.

Kwame Nkrumah University of Science and Technology (KNUST) Alumni National Conference, Chicago, Illinois, USA, 2010.

National Association of Catholic Chaplains' Conference, Columbus, Ohio, USA, 2006.

Benny Hinn Miracle Crusade, Milwaukee, Wisconsin, USA, 2004.

Billy Graham School of Evangelism, Kansas City, Missouri, USA, 2004.

Archdiocese of Chicago Charismatic Renewal Conference, Chicago, Illinois, USA, 2003.

Trained Volunteer Tutor at Laubach Literacy Action, Chicago, Illinois, USA, 2003.

Benny Hinn Miracle Crusade, Louisville, Kentucky, USA, 2002.

Billy Graham School of Evangelism, Cincinnati, Ohio, USA, 200

Investment in Africa Conference, Worcester, Massachusetts, USA, 2002.

Connecticut American Montessori Conference, Hartford, Connecticut, USA, 2002.

National Catholic Charismatic Renewal Conference, Scranton, Pennsylvania, USA, 2002.

National American Montessori Conference, Atlanta, Georgia, USA, 2001.

Advanced Leadership Training for Christian Leaders in Developing Countries, Singapore, Asia, 2000.

Catholic Charismatic Renewal Leaders' Conference, Kumasi-Ghana, 2000.

Berekum Training College Old Students Association (BETCOSA), Kumasi-Ghana, 2000.

First-Ever Ghana Catholic School of Evangelization by Germany and Malta Teams, Kumasi-Ghana, 1992.

Ghana Scripture Union /Christian Fellowship (Ecumenical) - Retreats, Crusades, Camp Meetings, and Conferences (Ahafo Hwidem, Goaso, Sunyani, and Kumasi), 1975-1988.

Education

2004-2007: Catholic Theological Union (CTU), Chicago, Illinois, USA; Ecumenical Doctor of Ministry.

2005-2006: Claret Center, Chicago, Illinois, USA; Spiritual Direction International Internship.

2002-2004: Catholic Theological Union (CTU), Chicago, Illinois, USA; Master of Arts in Pastoral Studies (MAPS).

2001-2002: Clinical Pastoral Education (CPE) Residency, Saint Raphael Hospital, New Haven, Connecticut, USA.

1984-1987: Kwame Nkrumah University of Science and Technology (KNUST), Kumasi-Ghana, Bachelor of Arts (Social Sciences).

1972-1974: Berekum Post-Secondary Teacher Training College, Berekum, Brong Ahafo Region, Ghana.

1967-1972: Obuasi Secondary Technical (SECTECH) Obuasi, Ashanti Region, Ghana.

1960-1962: Kintampo Local Authority Primary and Middle Schools, Kintampo, Brong Ahafo Region, Ghana

1960-1962: Effia Methodist Primary School, Effia (Near Effiekuma, Takoradi Port City), Western Region, Ghana.

1959-1960: Bodom Presbyterian Primary School, Bodom-Nkoranza, Brong Ahafo Region, Ghana.

Employment History

2005-2015: Board Certified Professional Staff Chaplain, University of Chicago Medical Center, Chicago, Illinois, USA.

2014-2016: Ombudsman, Council of Brong Ahafo Associations of North America (COBAANA).

2013-2016: Missions Director, Ghanaian Catholic Charismatic Renewal- North America (G-CCRA-NA).

2010-2015: Representative of University of Chicago Medical Center at the Kenwood-Hyde Park Interfaith Council, Chicago, Illinois, USA.

August-November 2005: Staff Chaplain, Mercy Hospital, Chicago, Illinois, USA.

2003-2005: Registry Chaplain, University of Chicago Hospitals, Chicago, Illinois, USA.

1995-2001: Headmaster, Maranatha International School, Daban Panin-Kumasi, Ashanti Region, Ghana.

1991-1993: Headmaster, St. Louis Junior Secondary School, Mbrom-Kumasi, Ashanti Region, Ghana.

1990-1991: Diocesan Development Officer, Sunyani Catholic Diocese, Sunyani, Brong Ahafo Region, Ghana.

1974-1984: Headteacher, Catholic Primary School, Hwidiem, Brong Ahafo Region, Ghana.

1974, September-October: Teacher, Catholic Primary School, Ahafo Kenyasi II, Brong Ahafo Region, Ghana.

1974-2016: Counselor and Spiritual Director & Chaplain, Evangelist/Preacher/Conference Speaker, Volunteer Church Worker in Parishes, Churches, and Ministries.

Donations

Donations Accepted at http://donations.ghanarodi.org
Website: www.ghanarodi.org

E-Mail: *gabriel@ghanarodi.org*

gabriel.ab925@yahoo.com

gabrielabm1913@gmail.com

Chicago: Tel: 773-968-1983, 773-363-7889

Ghana: Tel: 020-812-1463, 020-783-0406, 020-783-0000

To Order Copies Of My Books In Chicago

Kilimanjaro International, Hyde Park
1305 East 53rd Street

Chicago, IL 60615

Tel: 773-324- 4860

Email: katumba2@alive.com

Xlibris Publishers

1-888-795-4274

To Order Copies Of My Books Online

Orders@Xlibris.com

www.Xlibris.com

www.amazon.com

www.barnesandboble.com

Available Formats: EBook, Audio Book, Paper and Hard Cover.

Rehoboth House Online Distributors

www.amazon.com

https://www.eden.co.uk

http://www.powells.com

http://www.audible.com

www.barnesandboble.com

http://www.christianbook.com

http://www.booksamillion.com/books

http://www.deepershopping.com/books.html

Available Formats: EBook, Audio Book, Paper and Hard Cover.

Author's Profile

Mrs. *Agatha Amoateng-Boahen*

The Controlling Power Of The Mind

Dr. Gabriel Amoateng-Boahen

www.ingramcontent.com/pod-product-compliance
Lightning Source LLC
Chambersburg PA
CBHW021638080526
44584CB00015BA/1539